39 Precious Gems

ON

"How to Walk with

The Master"

BY

KAREN JOHNSON

International Standard Book Number:

978-1-888081-89-3

Published by

GOOD NEWS FELLOWSHIP MINISTRIES

220 Sleepy Creek Rd.

Macon, GA 31210

Phone: (478) 757-8071

Dedication

<u>Dedicated to Oklahoma's 39 Native American Tribes</u>

In the scourging of Christ, there were 39 stripes to His body. With each stripe, a drop of His blood fell. I believe the blood drops could have been caught by angels who carried them to the Father causing them to be turned into GEMS of His love and placed in His crown.

There are 39 Native American Tribes in Oklahoma (home of the Red man). These tribal governments could be reserved by God for His end-time purposes.

Honoring the Native people is a joy. God's eternal "sure mercies" covenant is included in the 39 Gems.

Here are the 39:

Tribe of Judah and Tribe of Benjamin, Shawnee Tribe, Loyal Shawnee Tribe, Alabama-Quassarte (Creek) Tribe, Muscogee (Creek) Tribe, Apache Tribe, Caddo Tribe, Cheyenne-Arapaho Tribes, Chickasaw Tribe, Choctaw Tribe, Citizen Potawatomi Tribe, Comanche Tribe, Delaware Eastern and Western Tribes, Ft. Sill Apache Tribe, Eastern Shawnee Tribe, Iowa Tribe, Kaw Tribe, Kialegee Tribe, Kiowa Tribe, Miami Tribe, MODOC Tribe, Osage Tribe, Otoe-Missouria Tribe, Ottawa Tribe, Pawnee Tribe, Peoria Tribe, Ponca Tribe, Quapaw Tribe, SAC and Fox Tribe, Seminole Tribe, Seneca-Cayuga Tribe, THLOPTHLOCCO/Creek Tribe, Tonkawa Tribe, United Keetoowah Ban of Cherokee Tribe, Wichita Tribe, Wyandotte Tribe, and Yuchi Tribe-all of Oklahoma

FORWARD

Karen Johnson is a recognized International minister with a gift of a Prophetess and along with the gifting of preaching has put together this splendid book of truly spiritual gemstones, titled 39 gems of the Bible.

After reading the thirty-nine highlighted scriptures that I only wish I would have had the insight to write a book on these very important portions of God's Word. I can only say that this book will inspire you also as you understand that the bible as a whole is truly a masterpiece of our life written and composed by the Holy Spirit. And the reference scriptures as inspired by Karen to help us to understand the way that the Holy Spirit opens up our hearts to what we need to learn and to sometimes aid us in spiritual conflict that arises from time to time.

I only hope that you can discern that through Karen and her wonderful spiritual ability to put together so many gemstones of revelation to point readers to 39 scriptural passages that can help shorten our search to many situations we encounter in our Christian life.

That understanding alone is like treasuring the gems of revelation provided by Karen in this book that will probably be placed at your bedside as a provider of nightly reading from a busy world of spiritual conflict that we all go through.

There are probably thousands of books inspired to help us as we learn to live and overcome in our personal life searches from God's Word. I realized early in my spiritual life in Christ Jesus that I needed writers to help me understand the Bible and fight the good fight of faith that might have been lost if I did not have other anointed writers to help me win and overcome.

Karen's book will be that spiritual strength that will make easy understandable insight to scriptures that can become a source of great victories of warfare we encounter in this life.

I feel it is a great honor to be asked to contribute to this timely writing using the application of 39 gems as a reference to the scriptures of revelation that will be a part of our treasures as we venture on this great gospel road of the Kingdom of God.

I look forward to working with Karen as we serve to minister together in a future effort to bring proper reconciliation of many useless conflicts concerning Native Tribes in Oklahoma of history past. My desire is that Karen will use her gift of writing to perhaps in the near future write another book and report great breakthroughs in our efforts among, especially my tribe of Southern Cheyenne of Oklahoma.

The final word that is hard for me to explain in a sentence or a paragraph is that I have been involved in bringing the 39 Tribes of Oklahoma into the Kingdom of God. These are my rough crude gems that I know that God wants to polish and present to himself through His son Jesus Christ. I believe that Karen's book on the 39 Gems of scripture will lead the charge into my efforts with the 39 Tribes of Oklahoma.

Thank you Karen Johnson for your obedience in writing this book, that I know will inspire all who read it.

Apostle Jay Swallow

Minister to Native America

Table of Contents

List of Gems

Gem #1: Ephesians 6:10-20- Armor of God

Gem #2: Matthew 16:19- Keys to the Kingdom

Gem #3: Psalms 97:22-Authority to Loose Truth

Gem #4: Daniel 4:34-35; John 5:30-Surrender to His Sovereignty-HE RULES

Gem #5: Galatians 5:22-26 -Yield to Holy Spirit

Gem #6: 1 Thessalonians 5:18- Ask God for...

Gem #7: Psalms 91; Hebrews 1:14- Ask for Angelic Hosts

Gem #8: Psalms 19-Meditate on His Word

Gem #9:   Psalm s13:5 –Be delivered from Control

Gem #10:   Isaiah 11:2 -Trust God for revelation, knowledge

Gem #11:   Psalms 51- Ask God to expose heart issues

Gem #12:   Acts 2:38-Repent of Idols

Gem #13:   Exodus 30:23-25- Let new oil flow-get in His overflow

Gem #14:   Acts 1:8 – Ask God for lost souls and power to witness

Gem #15:   Ephesians 1:17-23 – Seek God for His secrets of silver and gold

Gem #16:   1 Corinthians 12:7-12 -Trust God for miracles

Gem #17:   Isaiah 60; Hebrews 3:8-He is the Repairer of the breach

Gem #18:   Matthew 6:33; Gal 1:12; Revelation 1:1   Seek 1st the Kingdom of God

Gem #19:   Revelation 4- Open Heaven-ASCEND

Gem #20:   Psalms 89; Psalms 110 – Jesus and Justice

Gem #21: Philippians 2:11-Seek to know His layered love

Gem #22: Matthew 26:36-45 - Experience your personal Gethsemane

Gem #23: 2 Corinthians 10:4-6- Cast down vain imaginations and arguments

Gem #24: Matthew 18-Stay on your knees in humility

Gem #25: Matthew 5:3-12 - Beatitudes-Disciple's heart

Gem #26: Romans 12:1-2- Renewing of your Mind to Christ thinking

Gem #27: Philippians 1:10- Discernment of who laborers among you

Gem #28: Matthew 9:36- Manifest His virtue, fragrance, compassion

Gem #29: Luke 4:18-19- Set the captives free

Gem #30: 2 Corinthians 5:20 -Choose to be Christ's Ambassador as Paul

Gem #31: Isaiah 50:7; 1 Corinthians 13:12- Keep my eyes my face on Jesus

Gem #32: Matthew 6:1-14- Press on to finish the race set before you

Gem #33: Matthew 6:16-18; Is 58- Fast in secret

Gem #34: Jeremiah 1:5; Is 43:10- You were born for God's pleasure and witness

Gem #35: 2 Corinthians 10:5-Beware of assumptions...

Gem #36: 1 Samuel 17; 21:9; Isaiah 14:13- Giants of SELF, fall down

Gem #37: Zechariah 4:8-9 Mountains are to be conquered

Gem #38: Isaiah 8:11-22-Fear of God is the beginning of wisdom

Gem #39: Psalms of David-Thanksgiving brings life and happiness

My Story

I love God--why you say? Let me tell you a story about God's supernatural love and grace. Ready or not--believe all things are possible if you choose to seek God with all your heart.

My Story began in my mother's womb. I was conceived after World War 2 in Baltimore, MD. Yes, my father suffered serious post-traumatic stress syndrome, PTSS, from Battle of the Bulge and the hedges of Saint Lo and yes, my mother suffered emotionally from abuse but was physically attractive. I was not wanted and my resemblance to my father's side of the family only increased my mother's rejection and the Gross family disdain. Over time, I grew on my parents with some favor. I chose to pursue academic excellence as my escape into the "world of the lost"--a career with my own identity. My parents divorced after 10 years of marriage and 3 children.

Oh, what people do not tell you about life and all its exciting twists, toils, snares, turns and the many temptations?

I confessed my faith in Christ publicly at age of 14 and heard the call to be a missionary. But I was truly delivered and born again spiritually December 26, 1986 in a 3-hour visitation by God to cross the great abyss by FAITH and receive Christ as my Lord and Savior.

Filled with the Holy Spirit in March 1987, I surrendered to His Lordship and was ordained in January 1995 by the Freewill Baptist Church elders by the laying on of hands. They read Isaiah 45 over me to do prison ministry and set the captives free. My life has never been the same since. Discovering my Hebrew roots has been life changing and exciting to go deeper with God and His loving Covenant of redemption for the world.

I do pray that God will bless you and the Holy Spirit will give you revelation into all the secrets of Heaven and promises to walk out your salvation to His glory.

GEM #1

Put on whole armor of God declaring its meaning in Christ and pray a hedge of protection (hedge of fire) around your family.

Scripture: Ephesians 6:10-20 says "Finally be strong in the Lord and in his mighty power. Put on the full armor of God so that you can take your stand against the devil's schemes. For your struggle is not against flesh and blood, but against the rulers, against the authorities, against flesh and blood, but against the authorities, against the powers of this dark world and against the spiritual forces of evil in the heavenly realms.

Therefore, put on the armor of God, so that when the day of evil comes, you may be able to stand your ground and after you have done everything to stand. Stand firm then with the belt of truth buckled around your waist, with the breast plate of righteousness in place, and with your feet fitted with the readiness that comes from the gospel of peace. In addition to all this, take up the shield of faith, with which you can extinguish all the flaming arrows of the evil one. Take the helmet of salvation and the sword of the Spirit which is the word of God. And pray in the Spirit on all occasions with all kinds of prayers and requests. With this in mind, be alert and always keep on praying for all the saints."

How to apply the word of God by faith: Picture yourself clothed in His very essence that fulfills His Word and defines who HE IS WALKING BY FAITH CLOTHED IN HIS IDENTITY.

Fruit that remains: The world sees you born again, righteous, truth bearer, person of faith and action, peaceful countenance and attitude, and a profound believer in HIS ways and instruction.

GEM #2

Bind the father of lies and hurl down the accuser of the brethren.

Scripture: Matthew 16:19 (19) And I will give unto thee the keys of the kingdom of heaven: and whatsoever thou shalt bind on earth shall be bound in heaven: and whatsoever thou shalt loose on earth shall be loosed in heaven.

KJV--Keys of the Kingdom to bind on earth and loose

How to apply the word of God: Take your rightful authority as a king/priest of the King of Kings —a son or daughter and BIND the lying demons and whisperers. Literally, verbally, hurl (throw) down the accuser who stands before the throne of God attacking you to test your character and ways.

Fruit that remains: FREEDOM in Christ to shout-Victory in your House, your temple. No trespassers', no destroyers, no liars can cross the bloodline of the true believer.

GEM #3

You must choose to loose TRUTH, JUSTICE, RIGHTEOUSNESS and HOLINESS asking for mercy.

Scripture: Psalms 97:22 Clouds and darkness are round about him: righteousness and judgment are the habitation of his throne. - KJV - Foundation of His throne and nature of God

How to apply word of God: Loose (free up) God's word and His angels by decreeing His word of truth, justice (Jesus is), righteousness and holiness.

Ask for His mercy in any situation as He leads you to declare it.

<u>Fruit that remains:</u> Standard established in the Spirit realm of the witness of belief that HE rules and reigns on high and no other.

GEM #4

Surrender my will, mind, heart, emotions, body, and spirit to His sovereignty-HE RULES

Scripture: Daniel 4:34-35; Psalms 85; John 5:30

How to apply the word of God: "Yield to HIM daily." As I bow my head to the Lord to seek His will for the day, I ask to be yielded and still to the golden thread of His divine will flowing from His throne and discipline of my flesh to lay hold of it throughout that day.

<u>Fruit that remains</u>: Inescapable JOY of the LORD fills you and people are drawn to the honey that pours out of you!

GEM #5

Yield my vessel to the control and leading of the Holy Spirit's character.

Scripture: Galatians 5:22-26 (22) But the fruit of the Spirit is love, joy, peace, longsuffering, kindness, goodness, faithfulness, (23) gentleness, self-control. Against such there is no law. (24) And those who are Christ's have crucified the flesh with its passions and desires. (25) If we live in the Spirit, let us also walk in the Spirit.

How to apply word of God: Galatians 5:19-21 (19) Now the works of the flesh are evident, which are: adultery, fornication, uncleanness, lewdness, (20) idolatry, sorcery, hatred, contentions, jealousies, outbursts of wrath, selfish ambitions, dissensions, heresies, (21) envy, murders, drunkenness, revelries, and the like; of which I tell you beforehand, just as I also told you in time past, that those who practice such things will not inherit the kingdom of God.

Fruit that Remains: POWER of Gospel and evidence that you have been transformed by the love of God's workings on your soul to love others with compassion.

GEM #6

<u>Ask God for divine order, divine timing, divine appointments, this day for this is the day of the Lord has made and be glad in it!</u>

<u>Scripture:</u> 1 Thessalonians 5:18; Ephesians 5:20; Colossians 3:17; Romans 7:25

<u>How to apply the word of God:</u> The aspect of praise that gives thanks to God for what He does for us. Ideally, thanksgiving should spring from a grateful heart; but it is required of all believers, regardless of their initial attitude (1 Thessalonians 5:18). We should be grateful to

God for all things (Ephesians 5:20; Colossians 3:17; 1 Thessalonians 5:18), but especially for His work of salvation and sanctification (Romans 7:25; Colossians 1:3-5; 1 Thessalonians 1:2-7; 2:13). We ought also to thank God in anticipation of His answering our prayers (Philippians 4:6), knowing that His answers will always be in accord with His perfect will for our lives (Romans 8:28-29). Also see PRAISE.

Fruit that Remains: Fountain of living waters springs up from the well of thanksgiving and praise.

GEM #7

<u>Ask for ministering and warring angels (sentinel and sentry)</u> to be loosed to do the warfare and preparation necessary to complete God's will for your life.

<u>Scripture: Psalms 91; Hebrews 1:14</u>

<u>How to apply word of God:</u> Call upon the Lord and declare His promises of Yeah and Amen to His everlasting covenant over your life. As you decree His word angels are sent out to prepare the way and part the veil of darkness bringing the Light of His presence

exposing the enemy's plans to destroy. Pray for all the plans of the enemy to be ABORTED in the situation or life.

<u>Fruit that remains:</u>   BUT GOD has made provision to drive out the enemy through the power of His blood and His Name! Shout, Shout and blow the trumpet in Zion for the horse and rider have fallen into the sea.

GEM #8

Meditate on His word and worship Him in Spirit and Truth daily.

Scripture: John 2:5; Psalms 19

How to apply word of God: Ask Holy Spirit to give you a scripture that applies to the prayer target/person and turn to it and meditate (wait for the Lord to reveal insights that apply). Look up meaning of words and discern the heart of God. Write out a prayer that reflects the context of the scripture and revelation into the root issue.

<u>Fruit that remains:</u> Hebrew word for hitting the mark is "Paga "–You will hit the mark and destroy the enemy's rights driving him back and cutting him off to any access. Peace comes when you have prayed the heart of God's will.

GEM #9

Allow God to deliver you from controlling religious spirits, false yokes and burdens, false responsibilities and assignments. Flow in the supernatural realm of God.

Scripture: Psalms 13:5; 1 Timothy 1:3; 2 Peter 2:1

How to apply word of God: Yield to the fresh anointing of the Holy Spirit and let go of controlling forces that have you bound and weighed down with falsehoods and false teachings. You are free to be all God has called you to be.

Enter His rest. No striving!

Fruit that remains: Peace and joy will be yours as you find delight in all Jesus has already done for you.

GEM #10

Trust God to give you words of revelation knowledge, prophecy, for individuals and pastors and ministers as well as yourself.

Scripture: Isaiah 11:2 and the spirit of the Lord shall rest upon him, the spirit of wisdom and understanding, the spirit of counsel and might, the spirit of knowledge and of the fear of the Lord;

How to apply word of God: As you willfully choose to seek His face and spend intimate time alone with Him God will give you specific assignments and words to impart to leaders.

    <u>Fruit that remains</u>: Major decisions of life and death can be experienced and a turning of the tide. When God says to SHIFT to a new day or new level or new direction HE really means it. Do not miss the hour of your visitation.

GEM #11

<u>Ask God to reveal any heart issues or hidden besetting sins in your life that are stumbling blocks for anointing to move through you.</u>

<u>Scripture</u>: Psalms 51: Have mercy upon me, O God, according to thy loving kindness: according unto the multitude of thy tender mercies blot out my transgressions. Wash me thoroughly from mine iniquity, and cleanse me from my sin. (3) For I acknowledge my transgressions: and my sin is ever before me. (4) Against thee, thee only, have I sinned, and done this evil in thy sight: that thou might be justified when thou speak, and

be clear when thou judgest. (5) Behold, I was shapen in iniquity; and in sin did my mother conceive me. (6) Behold, thou desire truth in the inward parts: and in the hidden part thou shalt make me to know wisdom. (7) Purge me with hyssop, and I shall be clean: wash me, and I shall be whiter than snow. (8) Make me to hear joy and gladness; that the bones which thou hast broken may rejoice. (9) Hide thy face from my sins, and blot out all mine iniquities. (10) Create in me a clean heart, O God; and renew a right spirit within me. (11) Cast me not away from thy presence; and take not thy holy spirit from me. (12) Restore unto me the joy of thy salvation; and uphold me with thy free spirit. (13) Then will I teach transgressors thy ways; and sinners shall be converted unto thee. (14) Deliver me from blood guiltiness, O God, thou God of my salvation: and my tongue shall sing aloud of thy righteousness. (15) O Lord, open thou my lips; and my mouth shall show forth thy praise. (16) For thou desires not sacrifice; else would I give it: thou delight not in burnt offering. (17) The sacrifices of God are a broken spirit: a broken and a contrite heart, O God, thou wilt not despise. (18) Do good in thy good pleasure unto Zion: build thou the walls of Jerusalem.

(19) Then shalt thou be pleased with the sacrifices of righteousness, with burnt offering and whole burnt offering: then shall they offer bullocks upon thine altar.

How to apply word of God: Total vulnerability to the Holy Spirits examination of your heart and its motives. Let there be full exposure the Holy Light of Christ to your soul-mind -will and emotions.

Fruit that remains: Transformation and continued use of your life by the Savior.

GEM #12

Confess and repent of idols in the heart that would take time away from God including SELF!

Scripture: Acts 2:38; Acts 3:19—Repent and return to God

How to apply word of God: Choose this day whom you will serve as in day of Joshua. It is a choice, a decision of your own will whether you desire to follow God.

Fruit that remains: Life abundantly versus death and decay is a daily choice.

GEM #13

Let new oil and wine from His throne be poured in to you as you wait in His Presence.

Scripture: Exodus 30:23-25 Take thou also unto thee principal spices, of pure myrrh five hundred shekels, and of sweet cinnamon half so much, even two hundred and fifty shekels, and of sweet calamus two hundred and fifty shekels, (24) And of cassia five hundred shekels, after the shekel of the sanctuary, and of oil olive and hin: (25) and thou shalt make it an oil of holy ointment, an ointment compound after the art of the apothecary: it shall be holy anointing oil.

How to apply word of God: Make Oil for the priesthood and anoint the leadership consecrating them to Me by making holy alignment with His covenant order and divine plan

Fruit that remains: The oil God led me to make has been to 35 nations and has brought faith to heal the sick and dedicate leaders in the house of God globally.

GEM #14

Ask God to show you the lost souls in your midst, who to witness the gospel with and/or share your testimony.

Scripture: Acts 1:8: 8 But you shall receive power when the Holy Spirit has come upon you; and you shall be witnesses to Me in Jerusalem, and in all Judea and Samaria, and to the end of the earth."

How to apply word of God: As you are faithful to go swiftly, let your feet run to the nations with new shoes and new boots, the anointing is in the going through the gates.

Fruit that remains: Relationship networking begins with going through the open door to share what only God can do to change a life from darkness to light. The Kingdom of God is built from living stones passing through the fire to reveal His glory.

GEM #15

Ask God for His nuggets of truth to share with divine appointments and expect God to hit the target.

Scripture: Ephesians 1:17-23 That the God of our Lord Jesus Christ, the Father of glory, may give unto you the spirit of wisdom and revelation in the knowledge of him: (18) The eyes of your understanding being enlightened; that ye may know what is the hope of his calling, and what the riches of the glory of his inheritance in the saints, (19) And what is the exceeding greatness of his power to us who believe, according to the working of his mighty power, (20) Which he wrought in Christ, when he raised him from the dead, and set him at his own right hand in the heavenly places, (21) Far above all principality, and power, and might, and dominion, and every name that is named, not only in this world, but also in that which is to come: (22) And hath put all things under his feet, and gave him to be the head over all things to the church, (23) Which is his body, the fullness of him that fill all in all.

How to apply word of God: Believe that God will fill your mouth with HIS words at just the right moment.

Fruit that remains: Seeds sown in the heart of the listener will not return void. For it is a promise from God.

GEM #16

Ask God for miracles and signs and wonders that would bring HIM glory.

Scripture: 1 Corinthians 12:7-12 But the manifestation of the Spirit is given to each one for the profit of all: (8) for to one is given the word of wisdom through the Spirit, to another the word of knowledge through the same Spirit, (9) to another faith by the same Spirit, to another gifts of healings by the same Spirit, (10) to another the working of miracles, to another prophecy, to another discerning of spirits, to another different kinds of tongues, to another the interpretation of tongues. (11) But one and the same Spirit works all these things, distributing to each one individually as He wills.

How to apply word of God: Repent of any unbelief and false teachings and doctrinal error against the spiritual gifts. Trust God to move by His Spirit. Ask to be a wonder, a sign and especially for a miracle.

Fruit that remains: Aaron's rod budded as a sign, Moses staff turned into a serpent, tumors disappeared by prayer of faith, cancer is healed by prayers of faith. Only Believe and expect God's word to be fulfilled and manifested on the earth.

GEM #17

Check the motive of your heart for actions taken or words spoken in relationships. There may be unforgiveness. Your heart may have grown cold.

Scripture: Isaiah 60; Hebrews 3:8; Matthew 18:21-35- He is the repairer of the breach

How to apply word of God: Repent of offenses with Godly sorrow. Watch the movie, "The Passion", until you get a breakthrough in your heart. And let the words of Christ touch your heart to forgive.

Jesus said, "Forgive them for they know not what they do."

Forgive 70x7 for every offense. Wash their feet with the blood of Jesus and release them to God.

Fruit that remains: Restoration and healing are evident.

GEM #18

Ask God for revelation knowledge into the mysteries of the Kingdom of God in my midst and how to unlock and apply them.

Scripture: Galatians 1:12; Revelation 1:1; Matthew 6:33

How to apply word of God: FAITH in Jesus Christ not the law pleases God not man. Salvation is the great mystery revealed.

Fruit that remains: Redeemed so that the blessing given to Abraham might come to the Gentiles through Jesus Christ, so that by FAITH we might receive the promise of the Spirit.

GEM #19

    Ask God to open and shut doors so as not to be led astray into unrighteous relationships or man's ways of thinking and doing by lusts of the flesh.

Scripture: Matthew 7:7; Revelation 3:20

How to apply word of God: Authority to ask, seek and knock for God to grant favor and clear path to serve. Also, our senses should be tuned into the spirit realm for ears to hear and eyes to see into the Kingdom of God in our midst. Have your antenna up—listening to His still small voice too.

Know what is good and what is evil in the eyes of the Lord.

<u>Fruit that remains:</u> Righteous living and behavior with understanding of God's ways are not our ways. Have Faith to ascend into His throne room and beyond.

GEM #20

Jesus and His heart for Justice--

King David had an intimate relationship with God and God gave him the covenant of Sure Mercies. David asked God for vindication from his enemies. We can do the same as Kings and Priests, with understanding of God's ways are not our ways, but can be. We have to acsend.

Scripture: Psalms 89; Psalms 110; Psalms 7; Psalms 72

How to apply word of God: Pray imprecatory prayers for God to move spiritually to reverse injustices in government, in your home and lives of the widows and orphans.

Fruit that remains: Deliverance of those from evil to hands of the righteousness.

GEM #21

Seek to know the length, depth, width, and height of His love as a servant.

Scripture: Phillipians 2:6-11

How to apply word of God: Your attitude should be the same as Christ Jesus.

Fruit that remains: Shining star reflecting back to the Father in Heaven that you are HIS child full of His love and glory.

GEM #22

Experience your personal Gethsemane: Seek His face for intimate prayer time linking hands with the Savior, Jesus Christ, the mediator and intercessor of the Kingdom covenant.

Scripture: Matthew 26:36-46

How to apply word of God: Dying to the flesh desires and its lusts will produce a desire to pursue holiness, righteousness, truth, and justice.

<u>Fruit that remains</u>: Obedience to the will of the Father is evident in your life and all glory is given to HIM who rules and reigns on High.

GEM #23

Cast down vain imaginations and anything that exalts itself above God.

Watch out for strongholds set up in the mind that are familiar but not Christ-like.

Scripture: 2 Corinthians 10:4-6: (4) For the weapons of our warfare are not carnal but mighty in God for pulling down strongholds, (5) casting down arguments and every high thing that exalts itself against the knowledge of God, bringing every thought into captivity to the obedience of Christ, (6) and being ready to punish all disobedience when your obedience is fulfilled.

How to apply word of God: Ask God for a covenant partner who will speak truth to you when you speak out lies or vanity.

Fruit that remains: Clarification from the unclean and clean comes to your mind and you begin to see clearly God's plan for your life and end-time harvest. Fruit will manifest.

GEM #24

Stay on your knees for Spirit of Humility to be in your heart in order to cut off pride and self- directed actions. To recognize and resist temptations.

Scripture: Matthew 18, Isaiah 14

How to apply word of God: Willfully choose this day who you will serve by spending time in His promises. Make a choice to walk humbly and submitted to the Master.

<u>Fruit that remains</u>: Maturity comes and strength to resist temptations from flattery, vain deceit, worldly-minded counsel, foolish behavior and ignorance.

GEM #25

Beatitudes—Disciple's heart

I encourage you to desire humility of mind with a servant's heart to love your neighbor as yourself.

Scripture: Matthew 5:3-12

How to apply word of God: Ask God how you can reach out to touch another with acts of kindness and be a blessing for you are blessed of God.

Fruit that remains: Seeds of love are sown to reflect God's heart to a hurting and lost world.

GEM #26

<u>Stay focused on continually renewing your mind to the mind of Christ.</u>

<u>Scripture:</u> Romans 12:1-2: 12 I beseech you therefore, brethren, by the mercies of God, that you present your bodies a living sacrifice, holy, acceptable to God, which is your reasonable service. 2 And do not be conformed to this world, but be transformed by the renewing of your mind, that you may prove what is that good and acceptable and perfect will.

<u>How to apply word of God</u>: Ask God to put a Godly buddy in your life that will be courageous enough to speak the truth to you when you speak a lie. Keep a journal of thoughts that run through your mind during the day and when you get alone with God address the lies by looking up the opposite in the Word of God. Memorize and speak out loud many times the scripture that replaces the lie.

<u>Fruit that remains</u>: Boldness and confidence in Christ in you the hope of the world.

GEM #27

Discern who laborers among you.

Be careful and discerning what you share what the Father has given you in Secret.

Scripture: Philippians 1:10 Paul was given much and so was John but it was not time to be made public.

How to apply word of God: Ask the Holy Spirit for permission to release any word or revelation given by God in secret. Bind the flesh from the urge to appear super spiritual or important with revelation knowledge.

Timing is everything in bringing change to a situation, place or person.

Fruit that remains: Perfect timing of the Lord destroys the enemies' plans and aborts destructive camp.

GEM #28

Let Jesus' virtue exude from you when in the presence of others. Let Him fll the room with His fragrance, virtue and compassion.

Scripture: Matthew 9:36

How to apply word of God: A surrendered life provokes God's Spirit in you to be moved to see people healed and to know Him in the power of His resurrection. Let Him fill the room.

Fruit that remains: Delightful experiences with the Savior manifesting precious scents of lavender, rose, honey, and much more to confirm His will being done on earth.

GEM #29

    <u>Set the captives free! Let go of self- imposed prison bars. The door is open. Jesus holds the keys. Jesus has set you free. It is your choice to believe it, walk free in Christ and live abundantly.</u>

    <u>Scripture:</u> Luke 4:18-19 "The Spirit of the Lord is upon Me, Because He has anointed Me To preach the gospel to the poor; He has sent Me to heal the brokenhearted, To proclaim liberty to the captives And recovery of sight to the blind, To set at liberty those who

are oppressed; 19 To proclaim the acceptable year of the Lord.

How to apply word of God: Believe by FAITH in Christ's authority; His name above all names; His blood covenant; His Word.

Fruit that remains: A life worthy of the words "Well done, My good and faithful servant." Fruit that remains reflects His nature and character to the world so that they might believe.

GEM #30

Choose to be an ambassador of Jesus Christ 24 hours a day, 7 days a week.

Scripture: 2 Corinthians 5:20 Paul was Christ's ambassador.

How to apply word of God: Be reconciled to God and become the righteousness of God. TRUST God to lead you daily.

Fruit that remains: Your mind is resolved to follow the Lord and do whatever He tells you to do.

GEM #31

Set my eyes and face on Jesus and not man or my circumstances. Let Him place you with gifting's and callings in the body of Christ of which He is the head.

Scripture: Isaiah 50:7; 1 Corinthians 13:12

How to apply word of God: Set your eyes and your face toward God and do not look to the left or the right. Be on guard for jealousy, competition, betrayal, and Jezebel (witchcraft).

<u>Fruit that remains</u>: Consistent and confident walk in the Lord on His Holy Highway without giving into temptations of this world.

GEM #32

Press on to finish the race set before you.

Pray through a burden until release comes from anointing of Holy Spirit or you are given a promise/scripture to decree and/or confirmed by 2-3 witnesses, it has been answered.

Scripture: Matthew 6:1-14; Psalms 91

How to apply word of God: DECREE the Word of God that He gives you out loud with authority in His timing.

<u>Fruit that remains:</u> Glory to God in the testimony of breaking through and into a new place, new season, new direction.

GEM #33

Get God's plan by fasting and praying; denying the flesh and soul and power to influence God's heart and direction.

Scripture: Matthew 6:16-18; Isaiah 58

How to apply word of God: Total fast with water as directed; juice diluted with water for 3-5-7-21-40 days as God leads for a specific purpose. Expect God to speak.

<u>Fruit that remains</u>: Fast in secret. Discernment and sensitivity to the Holy Spirit causes you to be in tune and not miss God's will.

GEM #34

<u>BELIEVE:</u> "I am a witness for the LORD!"

<u>Scripture:</u> Before you were born, I knew you …
Jeremiah 1:5; Isaiah 43:10

<u>How to apply word of God:</u> Embrace and live out the destiny God has designed you for in His Kingdom.

<u>Fruit that remains:</u> Proclamation of reality of living Christ, the resurrected Christ the one and only God that lives and breathes and fulfills His plan for all eternity.

GEM #35

ASSUMPTIONS, PRESUMPTIONS and PRECONCEIVED ideas are sin.

Scripture: 2 Corinthians 10:5

How to apply word of God: Ask God to reveal by His holy light any thought life that creeps into the carnal mind by assuming, presuming and preconceived ideas.

Cast down falsehoods, lies and high imaginations and anything that exalts itself above the true knowledge of Jesus Christ.

Fruit that remains: Mind set and focused on being single minded in Christ to fulfill His good and acceptable and perfect will.

GEM #36

GIANTS of self please fall down. Giants are to be killed and dragons slain.

Giants are to be slain. King David knew God's ways intimately; therefore, he was confident in God's ability to slay Goliath in him and through him.

Scripture: 1 Samuel 17; 21:9; Isaiah 14:3

How to apply word of God: Justice of God prevails when facing the enemy. God will vindicate us no matter how large the enemy may appear. God has your back. Pray for giants of self to fall—self-ambition, self-will, self-protection, self-righteousness, self-made, self-preservation and MAMMON.

Fruit that remains: VICTORY IN THE HOUSE! Positioning for the future victories is set by God. David's spirit man had grown to be bigger than Goliath 9' size. God made him a "giant slayer" for David walked with God.

GEM #37

Mountains of adversities are to be conquered, moved, leveled, climbed and overcome by His great grace.

Scripture: Zechariah 4:8-9; Psalms 24 Speak –"GRACE, GRACE, GRACE "to the mountain to be moved; Isaiah 45 break bars of iron at the gate.

How to apply word of God for breakthrough: Believe Captain of the Lord of Hosts is with you.

Fruit that remains: Open heaven is granted.

GEM #38

Fear of God is the beginning of wisdom

Scripture: Isaiah 8:11-22; Matthew 10:27-31

How to apply word of God for victory: God is one to be feared and one to dread not man. Do not follow the way of idolatrous people.

Fruit that remains: Trust in God and His ways; hold dear the testimony of the LORD.

GEM #39

Praise and thanksgiving prayers and music lifts oppressive attacks from the enemy sent to steal your joy. Joy of the Lord is your strength.

Scripture: Psalms of David

How to apply the word of God for blessings: Thank Him, Praise Him, from your heart. What are you thankful for today—health, wealth, life, success, etc.

Fruit that remains: Evidence of His covenantal blessings daily manifesting in your life.

Concluding Remarks from Author

I invite you to read over the scriptures and pray to be born again and empowered by the Holy Spirit to know the power of the Kingdom gospel of Christ our Lord.

God's Way of Salvation –

Romans 3:23 "For all have sinned and come short of the glory of God."

Romans 5:8 "But God demonstrates His love for us in this: While we were still sinners Christ died for us."

Romans 6:23 "For the wages of sin is death, but the gift of God is eternal life in Christ Jesus our Lord and Messiah.

Romans 10:9 "If you confess with your mouth the Lord Jesus and believe in your heart that God has raised Him from the dead, you will be saved."

Has anyone ever told you that God loves you and that He has a wonderful plan for your life? I have a real quick, but important question to ask you. If you were to die this very second, do you know for sure, beyond a shadow of doubt, that you would go to Heaven? (If "YES"—great, why would you say "YES"?

The Bible reads "For whosoever shall call upon the name of the Lord shall be saved". And you're a "whosoever" right?

Of course you are; all of us are.

If you would like to receive the gift that God has for you today, say this prayer after me with your heart and lips out loud.

Prayer of Commitment to Believe

Dear Lord Jesus, come into my heart. Forgive me of my sin. Wash me and cleanse me. Set me free. Jesus, thank You died for me. I believe that You are raised from the dead and that You're coming back again for me. Fill me with the Holy Spirit. Give me a passion for the lost, a hunger for the things of God and a holy boldness to preach the gospel of Jesus Christ. I'm saved; I'm born again. I'm forgiven and "I'm on my way to Heaven because I have Jesus in my heart. Amen

About the Author

Rev. Karen L. Johnson has been an ordained minister since 1995; prophet to the nations called by God to go in 2007 and share the Kingdom gospel with power and authority. She has been to numerous nations and praying for open doors for such a time as this. While in Europe God took her into His presence to see the Glory Fire of His Throne as is stated in Daniel 7:9-10. At the age of 50 her father revealed her Jewish heritage (German/Hungarian) that had been hidden from her whole life which answered her many prayers of being drawn to return to Jerusalem. She has travelled to Mt Zion numerous times and has had many translating experiences to the Wall to pray for the priesthood to know their Messiah.

She founded the Victorious Life Foundation in 1992 and the Center at Gracepoint in 2012. While in Austria on 7-7-7 she saw God casting His gold net for the harvest of souls with Holy Fire and restoring His Bride to deeper intimacy and "sure mercies of David's" covenantal roots. Do you hear HIS shofar blowing and calling you to be free in Christ the Messiah and to go deeper with Him? God is calling for Elijah's to come forth and confront with Godly courage, the spirits of Jezebel and Ahab that have robbed His bride of her intimacy with HIM.

She ministers in personal prophecy and prophecies to leaders and nations. Karen also moves in miracles, signs and wonders of healing power of God especially for those who have been traumatized and have mental distress.

The sound of RETURN and repent with Godly sorrow is upon us. Her favorite is seeing justice restored and lives transformed where injustices and captivity have prevailed. God's vindication is real. She knows that God is restoring His kings and priests to form one new body-His glorious BRIDE. She is a Watchman on the Wall decreeing Psalms 24.

Karen is married to Tom Johnson of Elk City, OK and they have 4 adult children and 6 grandchildren.

Victorious Life Foundation, Int'l

P. O. Box 1628, Elk City, OK 73648 , 580-821-2410
graceplace2009@gmail.com + www.thevictoriouslife.org

www.ingramcontent.com/pod-product-compliance
Lightning Source LLC
Chambersburg PA
CBHW060404050426
42449CB00009B/1900